Knife
Fork
Spoon

A taste of the Sheffield Cutlery Industry

By Julie Benz

The Genius carving knife here was handed down to me. The fingerprinting revealed by these distinctive marks is similar to the assay marks on precious metal jewellery.

The Genius characteristic mark used on cutlery and scissors continued throughout John Blyde's trading, until the 1970s. John Blyde's son is said to be the first man in Sheffield to have driven a motor car.

The everyday usefulness of the simple knife, fork and spoon, literally touches us all every single day, whether or not we consciously think about it.

It set me thinking of the cutlery trade found on my own doorstep, in Sheffield. My particular fascination with the cutlery trade comes from my historical business involvement with jewellery – cutlery and jewellery making share many manufacturing techniques.

I love photography and I love trying to understand what makes businesses work or not. So here's my view on the cutlery trade, its past, present and its future. It's served in bite sized chunks that I hope will leave an appetite for learning more...

Julie Benz.

Above: Thrift Cutlery

The Round Building, in Hathersage, for me represents the modern ideal cutlery making factory; the greenery of this site is in sharp contrast to the stereotypical image of Sheffield industry, with its grime, smoke and dark satanic mills.

A previous gasometer on the same site in Hathersage inspired the Round Building's distinctive and award winning design.

The company was set up in 1954 by David Mellor, who initially designed for Walker & Hall. In 1969 Mellor opened a London shop, but his ambitious plans for expansion here foundered. In 1973 he started cutlery manufacturing at Broom Hall Sheffield. By 1990 it had relocated to Hathersage, 10 miles away and opened its own shop there. Entrepreneur Mellor sidestepped the decline of the industry by concentrating on design and on a design conscious market.

Mellor also designed for the mass market, with his 'Thrift' cutlery, designed for government canteens. Mellor regularly won Design Centre awards. Today his work can be seen at V&A, London and The Museum of Modern Art, New York.

David himself died in 2009, aged 78, although the business continues to be run by his son Corin, employing around 15 people on site.

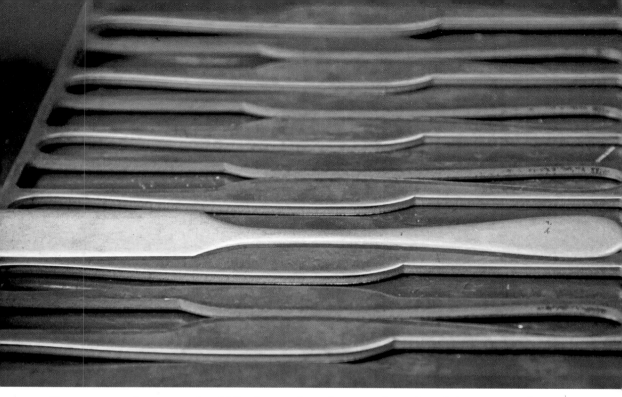

Shown opposite page: Steel blocks used to shape cutlery, involving a considerable force of pressure upon the flat blank, seen at David Mellor.

Above: The simple beauty of alternate pattern laying to minimise waste from knife blanks at David Mellor.

Illustrated overleaf: Left: knife blanks held up by workshop manager, Andrew Cisalowicz.

Illustrated overleaf, Right: spoon blanks, prior to being pressured and shaped three dimensionally using moulded steel blocks.

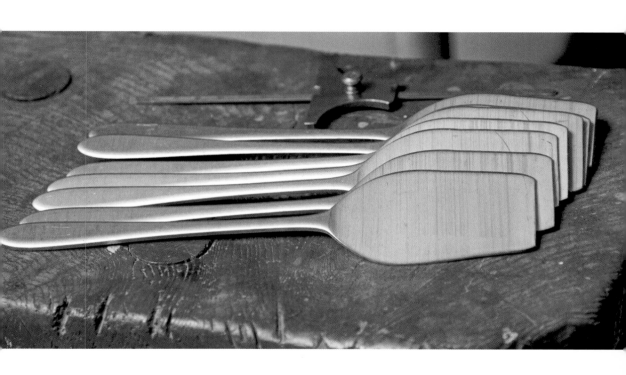

The Sheffield cutlery trade grew rapidly from around the 1830s through to 1920s. Trade was boosted by improved communications; the navigability of the River Don gave access to London via The River Humber and east coast and hence to overseas markets. Until America slapped tariffs on its imported goods including knives, Sheffield's knife manufacturers had had almost limitless demand at the peak of the UK cutlery industry, around the 1850s.

Savvy America, with its growing population, hence huge domestic market, conveniently protected its own fledgling cutlery industry through tariffs it set after its Civil War. It invested heavily in mass production, unlike Sheffield. Yes, there were a few exceptions, such as Needham, Veall & Tyzack, (later becoming Taylor's Eye Witness)- one of the pioneers investing in machine-produced cutlery in Sheffield.

Much is made of America's business driven culture, its lack of trade unionism allowing enterprise to free up. Yet Sheffield's cutlery trade, with its low skilled operations, its multitude of fragmented work sites – including outworking – as well its use of both women and children, were all factors preventing union organisation in the Sheffield until around the 1860s.

Top: David Mellor, Hathersage.

Middle: Tiger Works, West St, formerly Viners Works.

Below: Swann Morton, Owlerton Green.

The decline in the cutlery industry, after the 1920s, simply mirrored the wider decline of British manufacturing. Even in 1952 half the working population was employed in manufacturing, providing 25% of world manufactured exports.

By 2009, Britain's share of global manufacturing was under 3%, as manufacturing has moved to the developing world.

General reasons for the British decline are poor management, a failure to invest, outdated working practices, trade union obstructionism, the loss of the empire, along with failure to adapt to market trends.

The problem in the cutlery industry was exacerbated, because of the prevalent involvement of family members in the managing and ownership of cutlery companies. Short term profit taking through dividends were prioritised far more highly than investment.

Tweedale cites casefuls of cutlery family run companies, whose enterprising first generation built a fortune. In many cases, the second generation then spent this fortune. Among these an exception was the fabulously wealthy cutler George Wostenholm, born 1800, who married 3 times but didn't manage to have any children.

With no family dynasty on the cards, he sold the company a year before his death in 1876 to his business associates. So I guess the third wife got very wealthy.

The company declined around the first world war, clinging to its high quality pocket knives. Its size contracted and got bought out in 1977, but wound up being unprofitable in 1983.

My conclusion is that its product orientation- its lack of adaption to new markets -became its major downfall.

Ironically the largest cutlery firm of all in Sheffield was Viners, who were Jewish German immigrants, originally named Viener. In 1908 they occupied Tiger Works on West Street, before moving to larger premises. By 1970s competition from the Far East led to Viners importing its own Far Eastern cutlery to stamp as 'Sheffield Made'. This dubious tactic was not enough to save them and the company went into receivership in 1982, its Viner's name bought by a London cutlery distributor. Viners is now solely an imported brand.

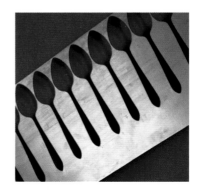

My conclusion is that Viners product orientation, by competing in the mass-market on price, was not profitable business.

Swann Morton is an interesting company structure. Launched in 1932, Walter Robinson Swann, in his words, a 'thorough going revolutionary socialist' and trade union activist, started making razor blades. The company claimed to be the first to introduce the 40 hour working week.

By luck the company was approached to make replacement blades for scalpel handles. Business boomed during the war with the demand for surgical blades. In 1964 the founders relinquished control in favour of a trust, giving 50% of shares to employees, the remainder to a charitable holding. Walter Swann died in 1980. By 2000 its turnover was over £13 million a year and continues to adapt and flourish, to the benefit of its employees.

Apart from Swann-Morton, of the few cutlery firms that continue here are Taylor's Eye Witness, Jack Adams, Arthur Price, David Mellor and little mesters Stan Shaw and Stanley Riley.

Interviewed by The Sheffield Telegraph in 2010, Geoffrey Tweedale, Professor of History at Manchester Metropolitan University Business School, explained that his directory of Sheffield cutlery manufacturers would ensure that the city's cutlery heritage would not be forgotten.

He began this work on the book in the late 1970s. "In those days as I walked out of the railway station the first view was of grimy forges and old cutlery factories. So many factories have disappeared and generations are growing up to whom the word Sheffield is no longer synonymous with cutlery." There are today probably around two hundred left working in the industry in this city.

We may need to look a little harder than Tweedale did in the 70s, but traces of the past he describes are still in evidence in parts around the city.

The first documentary evidence linking Sheffield to cutlery manufacture dates from 1297. Surrounded by hills, which gave Sheffield its unique advantage- water power- against other English cutlery competitors.

By the start of the nineteenth century, both a third of Sheffield's working population of 18,000 and also a third of all Sheffield's manufactured goods was involved in the 'American Trade', making fortunes for Sheffield merchants and cutlers. The trade inspired Sheffield factory names such as Atlantic Works, Washington Works and Columbia Works.

The craze for American 'Bowie Knives' from the mid 1830s to 1850s led to most Sheffield manufacturers capitalising on this boom. However, with the American Civil War, a hefty import tariff was slapped on imported goods, including Bowie knives and cutlery, which gradually forced British goods out of the American market.

Tweedale quotes from The Sheffield Independent in 1837, that thousands of these Sheffield knives blades were engraved with 'Death to Abolition'. Not very progressive. Apparently no record exists of American makers doing this.

The working conditions within the cutlery industry were appalling. In the mid 1860s the average age of death for a grinder was rarely above 40. Many died before they were 30. It seems to me that the modest investment and limited risk involved in setting up to be a Little Mester, as well as the involvement of women and children, aided the sweated labour, low waged and weakly unionised conditions found within the cutlery trade at that time.

Dixon's Cornish Place Works in 1893 employed 296 women and girls, 308 men and 66 boys. Tweedale quotes Conway, writing of Dixon's that, "Some of the girls may have once been handsome, but now the eyes brightness was a glitter, the only bloom was a flame."

Fast forward to my 'ideal' cutlery firm, David Mellor.

Above: I found the layout of work processes at David Mellor very visually appealing. The very traditional hand-written notes attached to the provencal dessert forks and spoons above, awaiting their plastic handles seems perfectly complemented by the dark grained wooden boxes encasing them.

Overleaf: By contrast these modern polished sleek dessert spoons to me perfectly flow without distraction from their black encasing.

The beauty and simplicity of their design is underscored when seen as a boxed set on the facing page.

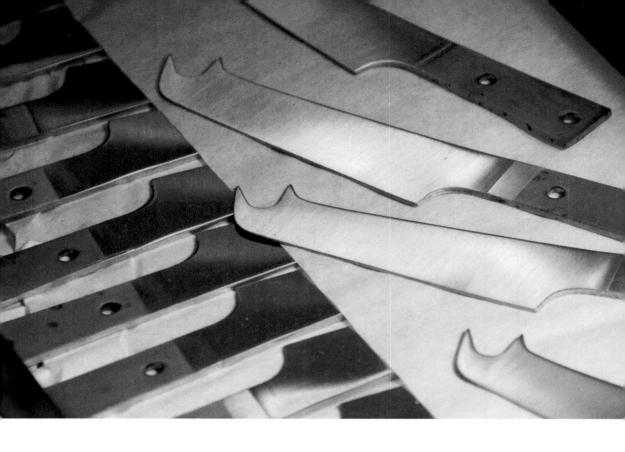

David Mellor

Someone needs to get a handle on these cheese knives.

For me, perfect form and perfect function above, showing the before and after of handle manufacturing within a shop display.

Before and after polishing stages, showing red and grey mops.

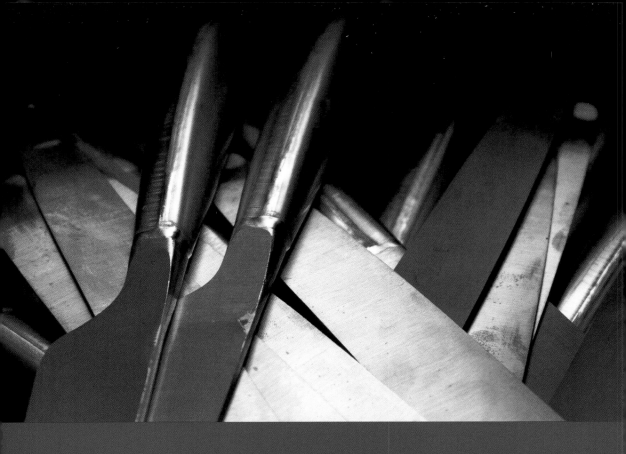

LÖSER

LÖSER KG

D-6720 SPEYER

GERMANY

OIL

GEARS, SHAFTS,
ROLLERS,
TABLE GUIDE
AND FOOT PEDAL
MECHANISM
DAILY

Stan Shaw is Sheffield's most experienced pocket-knife maker.

Born 1926, he started in trade in 1941.

After his last employer shut in the early 80's he set up on his own.

Although officially retired, Stan still works a couple of days a week, based at Kelham Island Industrial Museum.

Stan admits, 'Cutlers were never valued much in the old days. In fact you felt a bit ashamed to say you were a cutler, since it was regarded as very lowly'.

On this page Stan inlays a nameplate with a parser, a tool which he himself made to do the job. Previous page are shown Stan's files.

As all the ancillary trades have disappeared, Stan has adapted to become an all round man.

Above and opposite: Stan Shaw at work.

I was drawn to the hard working hands of Stan, as he showed me his current work in progress. The steel punch opposite punches the thumb grip on the knife handle blade and requires absolute precision and accuracy at the point of striking.

S.R Tableware.

The company was established in 1995 in a former scissor factory by Stanley Riley.

After working in the cutlery industry for more than 30 years, working for various companies, he decided to set up working for himself, in other words to become a Little Mester.

He specialises in bespoke tableware, available in sterling silver, but more usually made from EPNS, electro-plated nickel silver.

Although he receives enquiries for stainless steel, he laments that he cannot get hold of the steel blanks in the UK and thus is not prepared to pass off steel items as British, let alone Sheffield made.

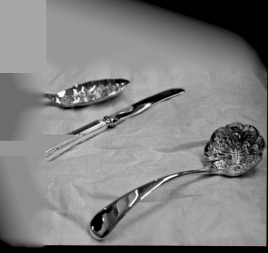

Left: Cranberry spoon which has been treated to prevent staining from cranberry juice, shown with knife and trifle spoon.

Below:
Stanley's work in progress hollow ware knife handles shown alongside the finished article.

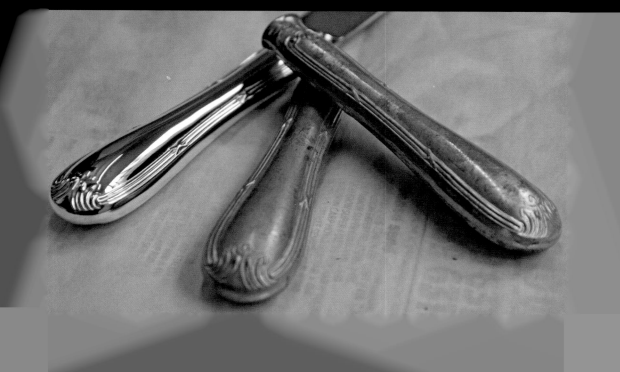

asked Stanley Riley about the timescale of making cutlery items. Just the process of grinding a dozen items, using a batch grinding method, in order to allow the metal to cool between different grinding processes, may take an hour.

He patiently distinguished between flat ware – solid metal cutlery as opposed to hollow ware, that involves a solid head, cemented into a three dimensional and hollowed handle, such as the three knives illustrated opposite.

Having worked for several companies that have gone into liquidation, Stanley has astute recognition of the strength of international competition in this industry. In his opinion the existing strong producers China and India will be replaced by Africa in the future; wherever the labour will be cheapest.

Above, opposite and previous pages:

Demonstration Open Day at Shepherd Wheel, illustrating hand forging.

Forging requires the metal to get to a white hot state, so used to be undertaken outside due to the poor interior lighting of forges.

Sheet punching of stainless steel cutlery (as shown on the front cover) was a tremendous technological advancement. It used mechanised machinery, superseding both forged and silver and silver-plated cutlery and suddenly made everyday cutlery affordable for all.

The innovation of stainless however coincided with the first world war, which almost overnight evaporated the luxury goods market, including 'for best' cutlery, high quality pocket knives and razors.

Similar examples to the grinding wheel shown above at Shepherd Wheel can also be seen at Kelham Island Industrial Museum.

The following two pages are also photographs taken inside of Shepherd Wheel. I do wonder how old the milk bottle is. Another everyday object showing that they just don't make 'em like this any more.

R.F Mosley & Company Ltd was formed by Robert Mosley, who started in 1861 a business aged 20, after being a scissor manufacturer's apprentice. By 1859 he had 240 workers at the Portland Works premises in Randall Street with the help of Mosley's manager, metallurgist Harry Brearley successfully trialled the making of about a dozen knives with his revolutionary 'rustless steel' alloy in 1914 – a milestone for the industry.

Mosley saw the future for stainless and thereafter marked their commercially produced knives 'RUSTNORSTAIN'. The company lasted at Portland Works until 1968. Half the company's workers were independent craftsmen renting the remaining small workshops at Portland Works.

IVORY & BONE HANDLE & SCALE CUTTER.

TURNER, CARVER & FLUTER OF IVORY, STAG, ZYLONITE, BONE & HORN SUITABLE FOR CARVERS. BREAD KNIVES, FISH EATERS & DESSERT KNIVES, DAGGER HANDLES, &c.

Columbia Works, 70&72 WEST STREET, Sheffield.

TELEPHONE No. 2774.

Above and opposite: Millennium Galleries.

No history found on Joseph Thompson in Tweedale's Directory.

Ivory and bone handles were very popular during the 19th century. Vast quantities of ivory was imported to satisfy the demand for handles. In 1878 Joseph Rogers & Sons used 2,561 tusks. Even by 1901 Rodgers used 15 tons of ivory every year. However, the company had collapsed by the mid 1970s.

Opposite and above: Millennium Galleries, Sheffield.

Ernest Wright, son of a hard drinking scissor borer, established his business in 1901. The business expanded at its peak in the 1970s to 45 workers as well as 45 outworkers, making scissors, knives and expanding in to tool manufacture. Although the company liquidated in 1989, with the death of the last family member, the brand name of 'KUTRITE', registered in 1954, still lives on. The resurrected company is based at Kelham Works, Russell Street, owning a string of traditional names and marks.The tales, relayed by staff, of the last family members driving up to the premises, in swanky cars, to fill up with fuel, was "the most we saw of them". Whether or not entirely true, it vividly portrays a company that was cut out for the benefit of family members rather than its staff

Challenge Works, Arundel Street.

Built around 1880s, this was used as an edge tool manufactory and is now a grade II listed building. An electro platers shared the site around 1888. Tool forges were set behind the street frontage. Stamping machinery is noted in its listed building's description. To me the exterior belies the dirty jobs that were concealed within.

Green Lane Works, Green Lane.

Another exterior that belies its internal workings is Green Lane Works. Originally established in 1795 by Hoole & Company, manufacturers of ornamental stove grates, it was rebuilt with a decorative archway in 1860. Unfortunately the coat of arms previously displayed on the roof apex is now missing, as shown in this photo.

From 1930 to 1948 Green Works produced files, as part of the Ibbotson Group (who also had nearby Globe Works, discussed later).

William Ibbotson was castigated by Frederick Engels, in the Condition of the Working Class in England, as a manufacturer...

"who had made himself obnoxious by an active participation in bourgeoisie movements, by low wages, the exclusive employment of knobsticks (non union workers) and the exploitation of the Poor Law for his own benefit."

Neil Woodall 1994.

Not difficult to guess this location. Grinders Hill.

The roughness of the sculpture over the steps doesn't do justice to the grinders that had to be so precise in their own labours, in my opinion.

For me a more interesting sculpture is the 'cheese grater' car park, just seen at the rear of this picture.

Butcher Works Arundel Street

Photographed in heavily contrasting light, the black
and white version came out better.

Beehive Works, Milton Street.

Built in stages in the second half of the 19th century, this building is now Grade II* listed.

By 1888 the cutlery manufacturer Atkinson Brothers took over Beehive Works, successful enough to be listed on the stock exchange in 1897. Later it was taken over by Gregory Fenton Ltd, whose trade mark was a beehive. The company still operates from these works on a reduced capacity.

Current residents also include Little Mesters Reg Cooper, Bowie knife maker, pocket knife maker Trevor Ablett and grinder Brian Allsop.

Next door stands Taylors Eye Witness Works (not shown).

Taylors Eye Witness, knife makers since 1838, moved to the current Milton Street premises in 1879. The company was one of the pioneers of machine-produced cutlery in Sheffield, being aware of the threat of German competition. Recent products include Sabatier knives and scissors.

The company's Eye of Providence, or 'All seeing eye' mark, which has masonic connotations, has been updated, but remains striking and distinctive.

Butcher Works.

Dating from 1820, these austere works were built by enterprising brothers William and Samuel Butcher. They remained active until 1959.

In its heyday, the company apparently employed 1000 workers. The large chimney in the yard was built to supply mechanical power to the works. As one of the finest remaining integrated cutlery, edge tool and file making works, it is now Grade II * listed.

During the 1860s some trade unions in Sheffield used violence against non-members in what became known as the "Sheffield Outrages." (see more, opposite page). Butchers Works was a safe place to work for those who opposed the unions, given that access was only through a single guarded door, shown as a black and white photo on page 53.

Steel production's unpleasant working conditions were described by Engels in 1844, in The Condition of the Working Class in England.

"In Sheffield the wages are better and external state of the workers also. On the other hand... certain operations require the constant pressure of tools against the chest and engender consumption in many cases...by far the most unwholesome work is the grinding of knife blades and forks, which especially when done with dry stone, entails certain early death...the dry grinders average life is hardly 35, the wet grinders rarely exceeds 45."

Sheffield became one of the main centres for trade union organisation in the UK. This culminated in a series of explosions and murders carried out by a small group of union militants, called the "Sheffield Outrages".

The Sheffield Trades Council organised a meeting in Sheffield in 1866 at which a forerunner to the TUC was formed.

Globe Works, Green Lane.

Cutlery manufacturers Ibbotson Brothers built Globe Works, in 1825, as an integrated steel and tool making complex, using steam power. It was possibly the world's first purpose built cutlery factory.

Its grand exterior contrasts with its previously grimy interior. Unusually, it was big enough to have a residential wing, with William Ibbotson's wife and large family living there until the 1840s.

With the decline in profits from American trade around 1850s, William became bankrupt. After his death the company became a steel, tool and engineering company, though no longer operating from this site. The company became absorbed by Woodhead & Sons of Leeds in 1939.

Tweedale, whilst lamenting the disappearance of many cutlery manufacturing buildings from 1970s until 2010 in Sheffield, worries whether future generations will recognise this heritage.

What I can see myself is considerable investment in several previously derelict cutlery workshops. I imagine that this has been made possible largely through acquiring listed building status, as a leverage for them to attract funding for renovation investment.

It is an interesting debate whether such vast sums of money can really be justified preserving, indeed fossilising, history in this way. Rather shouldn't money be channelled into industries that can actively thrive in future?

Arguably, such is the nature of grant funding, that investment goes to where the money can be raised, rather than where the priority is.

Admittedly renovation creates temporary labour during the reconstruction process itself and it makes for a visually richer architecture within a city that is largely devoid of historical buildings. Sheffield's centre and historical heritage, with its munitions industry a strategic target, was blitzed more than most UK cities during the second world war.

Other historical mill style buildings have been reinvigorated as factory shops or as apartments (such as Cornish Place) with private investment. As city living is beneficial for the vibrancy, safety, traffic congestion avoidance and economic prosperity of town and city centres, I'd personally rather see apartments as opposed to factory shops.

As for continuing to mark the city's cutlery heritage, there are fragments to be seen around – including contemporary sculptures, panels and signs within the city centre, shown on the following pages.

Along with the renovated cutlery buildings such as Shepherd Wheel, Globe Works and Butcher Works, I feel optimistic that the city's 'grinding' past will not be forgotten, even in the face of further decline in numbers of people that actively work within the Sheffield cutlery trade.

Above and opposite: Forkocactus Spoonelliflora. Steel. By Johnny White. Commissioned by Museums Sheffield 2008.

"Commissioned to celebrate ten years of Museums Sheffield, this sculpture is described as a kinetic donation box. As the coins drop they chime against musical instruments. The money collected supports the work of Museums Sheffield."

Well that's the official version. Johnny is a local artist, making sculptures and installations and you can also see more of his work in the Millennium Galleries.

This sculpture looks great, being inspired by the next door Winter Garden's cacti. But to be honest, I can't help thinking that they'd get more donations if it actually sounded musical when being donated to. Just a thought.

There are a number of other contemporary sculptures dotted across the city. For example Grinders Hill, near the train station, is a reminder of the concentration of grinders who worked knives and blades in this area in the past and another reminder is the cutlery panels on Arundel Street.

FEED ME

FORKOCACTUS
SPOONELLIFLORA
by
Johnny White

Above: George Ellis, Arundel Street.

George Ellis has a small mention in Tweedale's directory. The company became limited and was known to have traded from this address from 1932, lasting until 1971. Sheffield Museums and Galleries Trust has a collection of Ellis's silverware.

The site became more famous a few years ago, after Gordon Ramsey was called in to diagnose the woes of the restaurant, inappropriately then known as The Runaway Girl.

It didn't need a business guru and master chef to work out that Silversmiths was a better name. But given the fact that Silversmiths is still running, there must have been even more pearls of wisdom from the master-chef, that got put into practice.

Above: Cutlery panels, at the corner of Arundel Street and Matilda Street.

According to the Public Art Research Archive, the above panel section was installed on new build student accommodation around 2000. Surprisingly, neither the artist, nor who commissioned the panel is known.

Hopefully, I may find out one day who was responsible. It certainly brightens up an otherwise mundane brick wall.

Defining The Cutlery Trade

The definition of cutlery used by Tweedale in his Directory of the Cutlery Trades, that I've often referred to throughout this book. In his own words,

> " I have used the one (definition) offered by John Newbold, a 19th century director of Joseph Rogers & Sons. Cutlery in the strictest sense is the making up of knives, table spring and other kinds, razors, scissors and surgical instruments".

Tweedale continues that he also encompasses sheffield plate and other silver products, alongside ancillary trades, such as pearl and horn cutting. Tweedale excludes manufacturers of edge tools, such as scythes, saws and shears.

Tweedale then justifies this exclusion by continuing that, "some companies manufactured edge tools and cutlery, *but usually the line between these two sectors was quite sharp. They had a different culture, personnel and manufacturing techniques.*"

At first reading, I thought, fair enough. There goes the sad looking Russell Brothers photos shown on the next pages I thought, because its machine knives aren't defined as cutlery.

Then came for me a light bulb moment, after I picked up a copy of a book called 'More Sheffield Memories', which mentions a firm called Symmetry Medical-Thornton Precision Components. (SMI-TPC) It's not found in Tweedale's directory, as it no longer makes cutlery. Yet cutlery is where the story began for this company.

Today SMI-TPC is a major international player in the global orthopaedic market, employing 420 at its Beulah Road modern looking site. Yet the company started off in 1895 by George William Thornton with the help of his wife and brother.

Thornton's business was *'all about forging cutlery'*; it would grow to have some 350 employees. The firm comes across, despite the daily grime involved, as a paternalistic and generally good employer. To quote from the Sheffield Memories book,

> *" In the 1950s the company collaborated to develop implants...During the early 1970s with the decline of the cutlery industry Thorntons began to use more challenging materials and manufacture more unusual materials such as special alloys forgings for the aerospace industry.*

Hip replacement joints were perfected only in the 1960s by John Charnley, in Manchester. He found that joint surfaces could be replaced by first metal and later high density polythene, implants cemented to the bone. Now 95% of hip replacements are successful – a miracle of modern technology.

So Thornton's was well placed with new technology, innovation and adaptation at a time that its tradition market, that of cutlery manufacture, was in decline.

The current MD of the company joined as a trainee press operator, then aged 19. The company has continued to have an aggressive acquisition strategy, to place itself strategically as a full service provider. Along the way, the company invested over £6 million, from 1998 to 2004, using clear vision to secure a niche market positioning and having a constant willingness to invest in the future.

As at 2007, the company was anticipating a 25% increase in demand and cumulative investment.

In a nutshell, here's a company that was able to make a spectacular transition in techniques, away from its initial cutlery manufacturing starting point, in order to adapt and survive in a changing market.

So the difference in techniques between machine knife production and cutlery shouldn't be seen as a line that can't be crossed – and I'd suggest that the

unwillingness of the industry to see a wider definition for itself has been part of its own downfall. Adopting different manufacturing techniques didn't hold back Thorntons; it was able to make this transition. Thorntons even had cutlery as their core business until the mid 1950s. Surely there was time enough for strategic re-direction for others seeing the further decline of the industry? I think so.

Swann Morton similarly made a production technique transition, in this case with surgical instruments. For example, in the 1960s, they invested in a new scalpel factory, using the latest cobalt irradiation methods, to sterilise products.

In summary, it's a case of survival of the fittest. Or as Nicholas Comfort puts it,

> 'For every 10 British manufacturers that have given up, there are a handful of new ones driven by a thirst for success."

Matt Ridley expands this idea more globally. In predicting the importance in this century of a 'bottom up world,' where greater information sharing enables everyone to be better informed, Ridley sums up,

> "So long as human exchange and specialisation are allowed to thrive somewhere, then culture evolves whether leaders help it or hinder it, and the result is that prosperity spreads, technology progresses, poverty declines, disease retreats... knowledge flourishes..."

The market opportunities are out there for the thirsty. Now, more than ever, entrepreneurial companies and individuals may better understand where market niches may be through web networking, that can enable a more perfect marketplace.

The thirstiest companies will hopefully learn from the historical past mistakes by others, to improve their own chances of future success.

They'll also have to keep their knives sharp.

Julie Benz.

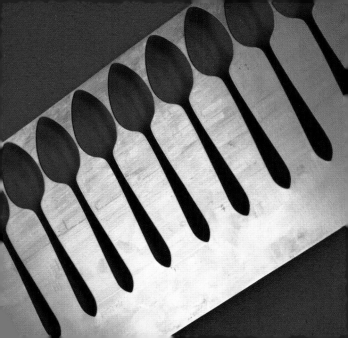

Further reading.

Geoffrey Tweedale, Directory of Sheffield Cutlery Manufacturers 1740-2010. (available online at lulu.com). 2010.

Nicholas Comfort. Surrender~How British Industry Gave up the Ghost 1952-2012, Biteback Publishing. 2012.

Matt Ridley. The Rational Optimist, Fourth Estate. 2010.

More Sheffield Memories. True North Books. 2007. (available from Kelham Island Industrial Museum.)

Further places to visit.

Cutlers Hall, (visits by appointment. Has a fine collection of knives and housing important trade mark archives)

Kelham Island Industrial Museum, Alma Street. Near Globe and Cornish Works.

Millennium Galleries, Surrey Street.

Shepherd Wheel, Whiteley Woods, open weekends 10-4 and Bank Holidays.

Many thanks to all those who generously gave their time to me for this book; Stan Shaw, Stanley Riley and staff at David Mellor.

Thanks also to Paul Iseard at The Famous Sheffield Shop, 475 Ecclesall Road for his wealth of local knowledge and contacts that helped my research.

I'd welcome any comments about this book.

I can be contacted at juliebenz1@gmail.com.

Overleaf: 1903 Old Ordnance survey map of Sheffield, extract showing Kelham Island and several cutlery works.

© Julie Benz, 2012

Published by Shaffron Publishing 2012

A CIP catalogue record for this book is available from the British Library.

ISBN 978-0-9568553-4-3

Prepared and printed by:

York Publishing Services Ltd
64 Hallfield Road
Layerthorpe
York YO31 7ZQ

Tel: 01904 431213

Website: www.yps-publishing.co.uk